D1017719

A 3-minute forever book

EAT
YOUR
PEAS®

for Sweethearts

By Cheryl Karpen
Gently Spoken Communications

To my Sweet Pea,

with love from,

At the heart
of this little book
is a *promise*.

It's a promise
from me to you
and it goes like this:

If you ever forget
how very **extraordinary** you are,
or
doubt for a single minute
how **grateful** I am
you
are in my life...

I promise to stop what I'm doing
look in your eyes
reach for you
and
remind you
with all my heart
how very much
you
mean to me.

In the meantime, there are some things I want you to know.

There's no better place to start
than to say

I love you.

My life is
richer and better
because of
you.

You
keep giving me
new reasons to be
in love with you.

How do you **do** that?

Isn't it amazing
out of the entire universe
and
all the centuries since time began
that we found
each other?

When I think of all
the wonderful times
we've had
and
the memories we've shared,

I can't help but
smile.

I love the fact
that we are
different.

I
wouldn't have
it any other way.

Thank you
for letting me be myself.

Thank you for loving me
just as I am.

I'm so glad you put up with my quirks.

What would I do without your grace?

Our love
will always have some
rough patches
along the way.

I'll be your **sandpaper**
if you'll be mine.

I know there are times
when I hurt you with
careless words.

I am sorry.
Truly sorry.

Thank you
for your patience
and
understanding
when life has been
less than perfect.

I appreciate you.

I believe in
your goodness,
your courage,
your strength,
and
your dreams.

I believe in you.

I love the times when we simply snuggle.

What are you doing this afternoon?

You make me laugh.

Don't ever stop.

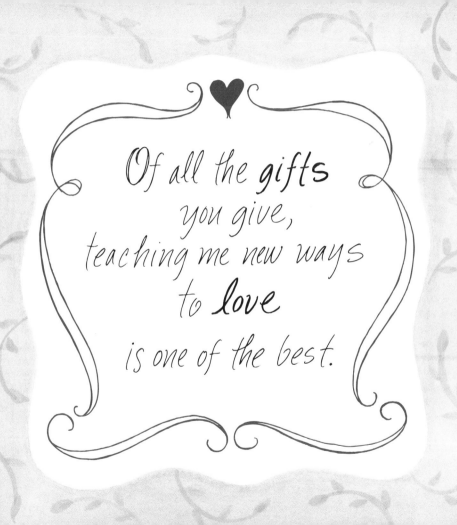

Of all the **gifts**
you give,
teaching me new ways
to **love**
is one of the best.

I love
imagining
creating
and
dreaming
with you.

Even when we're
not together
you are never far
from my
thoughts.

Fireworks
on the
Fourth of July
don't
hold a candle
to
you.

I love you
more each day.

I love us.

Our relationship
is a
rare gift.

Let's unwrap it
over and over again.

May we always
bless one another

with compassion

encouragement

tenderness.

And love.

Here's to us...

everything we are
to each other
and
all we are becoming!

Living our dreams...
Growing
together...

Just like

two peas in a pod.

Why Peas?

She was a vibrant, dazzling young woman with a promising future.
Yet, at sixteen, her world felt sad and hopeless.

I was living over 1800 miles away and wanted to let this very special young person in my life know I would be there for her across the miles and through the darkness. I wanted her to know she could call me any time, at any hour, and I would be there for her. And I wanted to give her a piece of my heart she could take with her anywhere—a reminder she was loved.
Really loved.

Her name is Maddy and she was the inspiration for my first PEAS book, Eat Your Peas for Young Adults. At the very beginning of her book I made a place to write in my phone number so she knew I was serious about being available. And right beside the phone number I put my promise to listen—really listen—whenever that call came.

Soon after the book was published, people began to ask me if I had the same promise and affirmation for adults. I realized it isn't just young people who need to be reminded how truly special they are. We all do.

Today Maddy is thriving and giving hope to others in her life.
If someone has given you this book, it means you are pretty special
to them and they wanted to let you know. Take it to heart.

Believe it, and remind yourself often.

Wishing you peas and plenty of joy,

Cheryl Karpen

P.S. If you are wondering why I named the collection, Eat Your Peas...it's my way of saying, "Stay healthy. I love and cherish you. I want you to live **forever**!"

A portion of the profits from the
Eat Your Peas Collection
will benefit empowerment programs
for youth and adults.

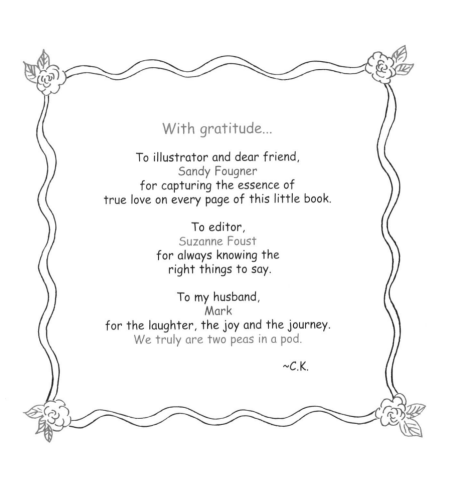

With gratitude...

To illustrator and dear friend,
Sandy Fougner
for capturing the essence of
true love on every page of this little book.

To editor,
Suzanne Foust
for always knowing the
right things to say.

To my husband,
Mark
for the laughter, the joy and the journey.
We truly are two peas in a pod.

~C.K.

About the author

"Eat Your Peas"

A self-proclaimed dreamer, Cheryl
spends her time imagining and creating
between the historic river town of Anoka, Minnesota
and the seaside village of Islamorada, Florida.

An effervescent speaker, Cheryl brings inspiration,
insight, and humor to corporations,
professional organizations and churches.
Learn more about her at: www.cherylkarpen.com

About the illustrator

Sandy Fougner artfully weaves
a love for design, illustration and
interiors with being a wife
and mother of three sons.

Other books by Cheryl Karpen

The Eat Your Peas Collection™
Takes only 3-minutes to read but you'll want to hold on to it forever!

Eat Your Peas for Daughters
Eat Your Peas for Sons
Eat Your Peas for Mothers
Eat Your Peas for Someone Special
Eat Your Peas for Tough Times
Eat Your Peas for Teens
Eat Your Peas for Grandkids
Eat Your Peas for Girlfriends
Eat Your Peas for Me
Eat Your Peas for Sisters
Eat Your Peas for New Moms

New titles are SPROUTING up all the time!

Heart and Soul Collection
To Let You Know I Care
Hope for a Hurting Heart
Can We Try Again? Finding a way back to love

To view a complete collection, visit us on-line at **www.eatyourpeas.com**

Eat Your Peas® for Sweethearts

Copyright 2005, Cheryl Karpen

Printed in the USA

For more information or to locate a store near you, contact:
Gently Spoken
PO Box 245
Anoka, MN 55303

Toll-free 1-877-224-7886 or visit us on-line at
www.eatyourpeas.com